Marketing on the Move

TABLE OF CONTENTS

Chapter 1 – Locating Trends

What's Hot Online Changes At Light Speed

New Internet marketing tools are coming online each and every day. Why should you care? Mainly because these new marketing trends and tools can have a dramatic impact on your online traffic, leads and sales. So much so, your online competitiveness can greatly depend on you finding and using these new marketing tools before everyone else does.

As Internet marketing grows more and more lucrative, it is becoming more competitive each day, so staying on top of what's happening in the industry has become vital to your online success. More importantly, if you're a full-time marketer like me, your livelihood will largely depend upon you being able to keep on up with of all the new ways of marketing on the web.

Again profiting from hot trends is only one of the newer ways you can leverage the power of the Internet. And as new ways to make money come online, others go by the wayside. There is no way to tell how long one money making method will last when it may be replaced by another.

So while profiting from hot trends appears to be something that will be with us for a good while (At least a year or two?), as fast as things change, you would be wise to not put all your eggs in this basket or any one online money making method. But that doesn't mean you get so many types of money making methods in play that you end up with none of them producing for you.

At the same time you need to start taking advantage of these marketing methods ASAP before too many people actually do see the profitability potential and the shear amount of competition starts eating into your returns for the time invested.

It will take some vision, forethought and planning to put yourself in a position whereby your potential competition will see your efforts as being pervasive and dominant in leveraging hot trends. Just like with many of the Internet Marketing methods you find where 4 or 5 marketers dominate those methods and you say to yourself, "They've got the market cornered on using this method", people will be saying that about you.

So lets seriously consider forethought and planning.

Vision And Planning Can Put You On Top

Plan your work and work your plan. You have probably heard that phrase a thousand times. But it has never been more true than it will be with setting up this, 'profiting from hot trends', system in such a way that you can implement it quickly and regularly as you find hot trends to capitalize upon.

Yes this system includes the plan to work this system effectively. However I am assuming you are approaching your Internet Marketing business with an overall plan with the primary goal of not just making money or generating revenues, but being profitable at it.

Some people will set down with this information and absorb it all in one day, and have their system up and operational in 2 days. That is what I would call a quick start. DO NOT think you have to do that yourself if you really don't have the time, study habits, computer skills or Internet literacy to become accomplished at using this system in just a few days or even a week.

The advice in this guide assumes that you are managing or approaching your business in a professional manner by having established long term goals, short term goals and are implementing the daily task (As you currently understand them), to attain your goals.

If this assumption is not correct, once you have read this project guide through completely and you believe it may take you more time to set up your system and start using it than I have estimated in my description of a "Quick Start", at least set some short term goals and break them down into the daily tasks it will take to meet your short term goals. That way you stay on track to having your profiting from hot trends system in place in no more than a couple of weeks.

You will need to integrate using this profiting from hot trends system into your Internet Marketing Business Plan so you can spend about 5 to 10 man hours learning and setting up the system and then committing one hour a day for as many or few days you choose to incorporate profiting from hot trends into your regular daily work schedule.

Planning Pays Big Dividends

Without knowing exactly where you want to go, how can you possibly expect to end up exactly where you want to be without a map or plan that will allow you to get where you want to be. Planning will also allow you to expend the least amount of time, effort and for some, even money to get there.

Once your system is set up properly, you're comfortable with it and you have made a couple of test runs, it shouldn't take you more than an hour to have everything you need in place to start capitalizing on a hot trend project.

Your hour will follow this abbreviated time line:

1. 20 minutes: Researching Trends for viability
2. 10 minutes: Locate keyword heavy copy
3. 10 Minutes: Set up your free blog
4. 10 Minutes: Monetize your blog
5. 20 Minutes: Promote your blog through back links

Obviously this timeline is a approximation and some steps will take a little longer and some a shorter amount of time. There are a number of variables that will come into play with each hot trend you decide you might profit from.

Just as obviously, in the beginning you will certainly take more than an hour to feed a hot trend into your system, but based on my experience I believe you can get your hot trends into your system in about and hour by the time you have done 4 or 5 hot trends. Set yourself a goal of being able to do it in an hour. If you always take longer, say an hour and a half or even two hours, you can still see a profitable return for your time spent.

One of the variables that will have a definite affect on your project completion time is the type of trend it is and whether or not you incorporate some of the optional or alternate promotion methods or strategies. That will depend largely on what you estimate the potential life of a hot trend to be.

Regardless of whether your research to deployment takes you one hour or more, having the tools in place to organize your system in one place will help you to cover the necessary steps in as little time as possible.

Getting Organized From The Get Go

As with any marketing system there are certain things you need to have in place so your campaign can be built and launched in as timely a manner as possible. The less time you have to spend on getting your campaign launch ready, the more time you will have to spend on other money making efforts and therefore more potential return on the time invested.

Any tool that can help you to organize your hot trend profit system campaigns will ultimately save you time. Your time is worth money. So lets save some money so more of what we make is profit.

All of the organizational tools you will need for your hot trends profit system are available online as free downloads or free web based services where you just need to sign up for an account.

Below are links to the free downloads you will need to build your system. If you already have some of these programs in place that's good. You may be able to use them as is or you may want to set them up separate from your current software in your program files in a different directory. This first list is software. The second list down will be free web services.

Tools You Will Need

The FireFox Web Browser:

We will be using Mozilla's FireFox Browser for a number of reasons including it is more secure than I.E. but more so because of it's plugin Addons that will help you organize your system with blazing speed.

If you don't already have FireFox running on your computer, you can download it here: http://www.mozilla.com/ click on the big green download button and save it to a folder you will or have named: @ProfitTrendsSoftware - the @ sign will move the folder alphabetically to the top and make it easier to get to when we start setting up your programs. WARNING: DO NOT SET THIS UP until you get to the "It's All Browser Based" section of Chapter 3

Free Service Account's and Tools You Will Need

A "My GOOGLE" Account:

If you already have a GOOGLE account, you will want to set up another one just for your hot trends projects. If you already have an account, you will need to sign up with a different e-mail address. Even if you have a Gmail account set up you should set up a new Gmail account. The purpose being you want to keep everything in this account separate from any other information you store online. It is cleaner and easier that way.

Just go to: www.google.com/accounts/NewAccount and sign up. You will be sent information at your Gmail account (If you already have an account) or your alternate e-mail account. NOTE: from time to time GOOGLE changes their mode of operations as far as these sign ups go so you may have to use a little common sense to read between their lines to get a new account.

Most of the tools you will use with this system will be from GOOGLE. To access any of the tools referred to from here on, (Before you bookmark them), just sign into your Google account home page and click on the tool icon of the tool you want to work with. You can also reach your account home page by using this link: www.google.com/accounts/ManageAccount

Login Database Tool

You will be required to enter a username and password when you sign up. You will be signing up for several free services. If you don't have a login info database like RoboForm you need to get one. It will save you untold frustration, time and probably your sanity. You can get it here: http://www.roboform.com/ there is a free version but it only holds login information for 10 logins. You'll need far more than that. In a perfect world you could just use the same username and password for all accounts but that's just not the way it works online. Some will assign your a password. Some will want a user name, some will use your e-mail address as your username.

Login Database Tool - A Free Option: You can use the "AllPass" database for login info. You can get it here: www.LastPass.com It is by no means the user friendly, feature rich and powerful of a tool that RoboForm is, but you can get by with it for now.

There are numerous tools from GOOGLE you will use when we get into setting up your system. When you are logged into your Google account, all Google tools will be available through the same account and you should not be required to login to use any Google tool unless you have logged out. The only services that run contrary to that rule are AdSense and Adwords.

Use Gmail for all Your Hot Trends Projects E-mail

The first thing you want to do is set up your Google e-mail account on Gmail. That is Google's Free Web Based e-mail. From your Google account home page You may have to click on "My Account" in the upper right of the page), click on the Gmail link/icon in the Products section. Configure your e-mail account any way you want.

It is VERY IMPORTANT to use this Gmail account for all the free services you will use for this system. Doing so will keep all your e-mail information apart from non Hot Trends related e-mail and you will be able to organize this e-mail account just for hot trends related communications.

Organizing Your Trends System

You are going to need to keep records of your Hot Trends Profits projects.

When you are on your Google "My Account" page, you will see an icon in the Products section that says "Google Docs". Click on that icon. It will load the Google Docs home page.

You will have the ability to use and save spread sheets and word processor documents for your system as you database information on your different hot trend products. If you understand Microsoft Excel, you can use the spread sheet documents to organize your project data. If not, you can use the word publisher document to paste text data information into in the most organized manner you are comfortable with.

I won't be showing you how to set up your data documents. Those kinds of things are always a matter of personal preference. You will only have about 6 distinct data items you will want to have available to you at any given time, so I'm not talking about mountains of data here. Still you need to have the someplace where you can get to them right in your browser and not have to go digging through your computer file manager to find what you need.

Another tool you will find on your Google "My Account" page is "My Notebook". Very handy for jotting down quick notes and keeping them organized where you can access them quickly as you are working your hot trends business.

When we get to setting up your Google Hot Trends bookmarks, I'll have you bookmark them accordingly. For now, if you want to take a minute and go check them out - you rock on. I'll be here when you get back :o)

In fact as you get introduced to any of these tools and get them bookmarked into your system so they are ready for easy access, you should take a couple of minutes to check out each one of them. Spend a few minutes clicking around on different menu items, links, help sections or FAQ's. Doing so may save you some frustration later.

If you don't already have the FREE browser we'll use for our hot trends system, we'll get it installed, set up and then configured for your hot trends projects.

Chapter 2 – Getting Started

Browser Set Up

Setting Up FireFox

If you already have FireFox set up that's great. If not, please go to the folder where you saved the install program and install FireFox. During or just after the install it will ask you whether or not you want FireFox to be your default Browser. It is NOT necessary that it is your default browser. If you want to keep I.E. or whatever other browser as your default Browser, just check the "Don't ask me again" box and click NO. If you do, click yes.

SEO for FireFox Add On

Now that you have FireFox installed, open the program if it is not already and go to:

http://tools.seobook.com/firefox/seo-for-firefox.html and download the SEO for FireFox add on. scroll down the page for install instructions.

Google Tool Bar for FireFox Add On

Go here: https://addons.mozilla.org and in the search field at the top of the page, search for "Google Toolbar". Install the tool bar. FireFox will walk you through the process. You may need to sign up for a Google account to get this tool bar. It's been a while so; sorry I don't remember. If you do that's fine, you will have to anyway. If you already have a Google account, set up a separate Google account for the purposes of this system. Google will allow you several accounts.

Don't Get Carried Away

There are hundreds of FireFox Add On's but for our purposes you only need these two. any more and things can get confusing. Not to mention the fact that you can get lost and or loose track of time cruising all the Add On's that are available. Let's stick to business.

Now Set Up Your Bookmarks Toolbar

When you save a link in Internet Explorer in your "Favorites" are called "Favorites". In Mozilla the same feature is available to accomplish the same purpose, but instead you save links to what's called your Bookmarks and those saved links are called bookmarks. In FireFox you can set up different a "Bookmarks Toolbar" button for different categories of sites with different purposes. Therefore you can keep all of your hot trends related sites in one Toolbar button. Click on the button and you will only see the sites links or bookmarks you have save to that "Bookmarks Toolbar" button.

To make sure your "Bookmarks Toolbar" is visible, just right click as shown in the following screenshot. If "Bookmarks Toolbar" is not checked in the drop down, click/select it and it will appear on as one or more buttons in the header of FireFox GUI (Graphical User Interface).

In FireFox, click on "Bookmarks" at the top of the browser then click on "<u>Organize Bookmarks</u>".

When Mozilla opens up your bookmarks data it will be titled "Library" on the Title Bar.

Right click on "Bookmarks Toolbar" as shown above and select "New folder..." by left clicking on "New folder...". Now follow the directions in red in the screenshot of the new folder dialogue window below, an naming the folder Hot Trends:

If you were to close the "Library" window now, you would see a new tab has appeared on your "Bookmarks Toolbar" named "Hot Trends". When you click on it, it will of course be empty because we haven't saved any page links to it yet.

Now let's set up more folder/tabs on your "Bookmarks Toolbar" exactly the same way you did Hot Trends. They will be set up and named in this order:

1. Hot Trends (You've already set up)
2. HT Blogs
3. SB Sites
4. SN Sites
5.

Now we will want to set our Hot Trends business home page, research pages and tracking pages into our Hot Trends "Bookmarks Toolbar" tab. But first we need to set them up on your iGOOGLE.

Customizing Your Hot Trends iGoogle Page
Ok, now that we have the Add On's set up in FireFox along our initial bookmark tabs, let's set up your default home page.

Assuming you have set up a separate or new Goocle account, Go to GOOGLE at www.google.com and login. Just click on "Sign In" in the top right hand corner of the page.

Once you are logged in click on "My Account" In the top right hand corner of this page. That will deliver your main account product set up features page.

Most will go in your Hot Trends folder/tab but not all. Just follow the instructions for each folder/tab as we go. Now bookmark your Google "My Account" page into your Hot Trends folder/tab.

Book mark all of the following pages into your "Bookmarks Toolbar" Hot Trends folder in the following order:

In your FireFox Browser, go to:

Hot Trends

www.google.com/trends/hottrends

Google Trends

http://google.com/trends (Different in that it will allow you to compare trend sites instead of just listing hot trends of the day.)

Insights

www.google.com/insights/search/

Checkout Trends

https://www.google.com/search?q="Hot+Trends"

Google Sets

http://www.googleguide.com/labs.html

Google Alerts

http://www.google.com/alerts

Now let's set up your Blogger Blogs Tab.

Loading Your Blogger Tab

Now you need to set up a tab where you will keep your bookmarks for your Hot Trends Blogger Blogs as you build them.

Refer to the"Browser Set Up" section at the beginning of this chapter if you don't remember how to set up a "Bookmarks Toolbar" tab.

Name it what ever you like. I named mine "HT Blogs" to keep it short.

If you have a Blogger account, go to your account and sign in to your "Dashboard Page". Bookmark this page to your "HT Blogs" tab on your "Bookmarks Toolbar".

If you have not already signed up for a Blogger account, you need to do so now:

Go to: www.blogger.com/start

NOTE: You should have already set up a Google account when you signed up following the directions in the "Getting Organized . . .) section of Chapter 2, and though you have not used Blogger before, that Google account username and password will work for Blogger. In fact it will work for just about any Google service you use.

Now that your are signed in and viewing your "Dashboard" page, bookmark this page to your "HT Blogs" tab on your "Bookmarks Toolbar".

If this is your first account with blogger and you haven't used it before, I highly recommend you watch the video tutorial at the bottom of your Blogger "Dashboard" page.

For now you are done with this tab. You will load your different blog pages into this tab as you create them. We will create your first blogger blot later in this guide. But this reminds me, we need to take a little time to go over keeping your Hot Trends Profit system organized.

I will cover all other aspects of using Blogger later in this guide.

Staying Organized

As you set up your different campaigns, you will want to keep records of what you did, how you did it and what the results of each campaign were in the amount of traffic you developed and the money you made.

In an effort to keep your Hot Trends business separate from your other business efforts but still available at the click of a browser tab, I'm recommending you use Google Spread Sheets or Word Processor Documents..

Go to: http://docs.google.com Bookmark this page to your Hot Trends Tab.

Here you will be able to create documents you can use to track your campaigns and have them all available right in your browser along with your other hot trends Google pages.

You can use the word processor to create documents you can later download in several different file formats such as RTF, PDF, WORD etcetera.

Your spread sheets where you organize your campaign information and results you can export in numerous file formats including csv, text, Excel etcetera.

I will get to how you set up your campaign documents in the appropriate section later in this guide. For now we are just getting our browser system set up for maximum production in the least amount of time.

Always Be Prepared To Take Advantage

There is a lot to be said for keeping your business organized to the point you are always prepared to take advantage of an opportunity when it arises, or in some cases before an opportunity even presents itself. However there is more to staying organized to the point that your online marketing system is ready.

Starting a any small business venture will place unprecedented demands on your organizational skills! While this Hot Trends Profit system is not hard to keep organized, (The way I'm showing you how to do it), if you are the type of person who strives to organize his or her projects and daily schedule to achieve maximum efficiency, you can expect to make some pretty serious profits with this system. However if you are kind of hit and miss at keeping things organized, about all you can expect is hit and miss profits.

The point will really come home to you when you get 2 or 3 weeks down the road, and maybe have been paying more attention to your primary source of income; then you find some time to do some hot trends research, find something that has real money maker potential written all over it and you realize you haven't kept up your files,records, tracking, bookmarks or other organizational items and realize you're really not prepared to take advantage of the opportunity in the timely fashion that is required in this endeavor to make it profitable and you end up frustrated and maybe giving up.

It's More Than Just Record Keeping

Internet Marketing doesn't just require keeping clean records. You have to keep your computer up with proper maintenance so you don't end up with some MalWare or Virus problem. You need to keep your registry clean, drives defragged, security updates current, automatic virus scans scheduled etcetera.

If you are not in the habit of doing regular maintenance on your computer or your computer is running slow, has strange quirks about the way it works, take some time and look around on line for some maintenance recommendations.

Here is a link to some good information I found on maintaining a Windows PC.
http://pcsupport.about.com/od/maintenance/Maintaining_Your_PC.htm

You should also check out this site if you have any serious problems:
http://www.suggestafix.com

This maintenance list they have there is great. I run through this every Sunday: http://www.suggestafix.com/index.php?showtopic=27337

Make these things part of staying organized and prepared so your computer will be prepared to see you through your projects.

Chapter 3 – Using Google

Ok . . . so just what are these hot trend things?

In my estimation Google should have named their "Hot Trends" service, "Hot Fads" or "Hot Micro-Trends. Primarily because prior to Google Hot Trends, it was commonly accepted that a trend was something that somehow becomes popular within mainstream society over a long period of time. It is the direction of a sequence of events that has some momentum and durability.

However we are more concerned with tracking something that somehow becomes popular with a portion of mainstream society over a short period of time. That ability gives us the power to tap into that portion of mainstream society quickly to generate quick, passive income. By passive I mean there is no sales effort we personally make to receive an income from tapping into people that have "Jumped on the bandwagon" showing their interest in a certain fad or micro-trend.

In plain language, a trend is usually caused by the "Band wagon Effect".

The Bandwagon effect, also known as social proof or "cromo effect" and closely related to opportunism, is the observation that people often do and believe things because many other people do and believe the same things. The effect is often pejoratively called herding instinct, or the herd mentality, particularly when applied to adolescents or even adults having similar particular interests. People tend to follow the crowd without examining the merits of a particular thing. The bandwagon effect is the reason for the bandwagon fallacy's success.

The bandwagon effect is well-documented in behavioral psychology and has many applications. For our purposes we will be capitalizing the band wagon effect that causes "Micro-Trends, or daily trends of interest. The general rule is that conduct or beliefs spread among people, as fads clearly do, with "the probability of any individual adopting it increasing in direct proportion to those who have already done so".

As more people come to believe in something, others also, "hop on the bandwagon", or indicate interest in the Micro-Trend regardless of the underlying evidence. In short, the bandwagon effect creates buzz about a Micro-Trend.

What Are <u>GOOGLE</u> Hot Trends?

Unlike what was commonly accepted as the definition of hot trends that require time to develop from fad status to trend to hot trend, GOOGLE has probably single handedly changed what people think of when they hear the word "Hot Trend".

Google's Hot Trends is a measurement of Google search trends. It is similar to Google Trends and Google Zeitgeist, except that it is updated multiple times per day.

The service does not measure the absolute popularity of search terms, as these don't tend to change much over time. Instead, Hot Trends looks for terms that have rapidly gained popularity relative to their previous rank or the previous average number of times a term has been searched for on Google.

What Google's Hot Trends and other Google services like Google Insights and Googles Check Out Trends allows us to do is; identify items of intense interest online and make determinations as to whether or not those items of interest can be quickly capitalized on using a system that will attract large amounts of traffic to a monetized blog this system allows us to deploy quickly.

Google Trends - A Different Purpose Than Hot Trends

With Google Trends, you can compare the world's interest in your favorite topics. Enter up to five topics and see how often they've been searched on Google over time. Google Trends also shows how frequently your topics have appeared in Google News stories and in which geographic regions people have searched for them most. (Per Google - See "Source:" below.)

Here is How Google Hot Trends Works (Source: Google)

Hot Trends reflects what people are searching for on Google today. Rather than showing the most popular searches overall, which would always be generic terms like 'weather,' Hot Trends highlights searches that experience sudden surges in popularity, and updates that information hourly. Our algorithm analyzes millions of web searches performed on Google and displays those searches that deviate the most from their historic traffic pattern. The algorithm also filters out spam and removes inappropriate material. For each search, Hot Trends shows related searches and a search volume graph. The page also displays news, blog posts, and web results to give context about why a search may be appearing on the Hot Trends list. You can also choose a date in the past to see what the top Hot Trends were for that date by clicking change date.

Source: http://www.google.com/intl/en/trends/about.html I highly recommend you read this entire page so you are familiar with both and what they do.

So let's go look at picking a hot trend.

Chapter 4 - Research

Picking A Hot Trend

We've discussed what hot trends are in the previous chapter. However there are things you will want to consider when choosing a hot trend to profit by:

- How HOT is the trend?
- When or if the trend has peaked
- Can the hot trend be monetized?
- How long is the hot trend likely to stay hot
- Is the hot trend tied to something seasonal

How HOT is the trend?

Let's take a look at 2 hot trends and use some tools and common sense reasoning regarding the potential for the hot trends shown in black below to make money. (Obviously these won't be the hot trends you will see now as they change almost hourly.

Ok so we go to hot trends from out Hot Trends book mark tab and there is the big list of today's hot trends for the last hour. We see in position number 1 is Clement Hurd in screen shot ht-1. We see in screen shot ht-2 ablve in position number 12, Jessica Simpson.

The initial knee jerk reaction of the untrained eye might think that Clement Hurd might be a hot trending project. Now lets look a little deeper. When we click on the Clement Hurd link we see on the "Hotness Meter" this trend is at the highest: Volcanic.

When or If the Trend has Peaked

However even though the Clement Hurd hot trend is in the number one position and has the highest heat, his Google Search Trend chart in screen shot ht-1b below shows the trend having already peaked 6 hours ago. This is what I call a splash in the pan hot trend. It is not something that will engender mass interest. So I have no interest in making it a hot trends project.

The news items on the left below the chart were not what most people would call hot news. Basically a press release about this children's book illustrator books being presented as a play.

Can It be Monetized?

The blogs listed on the right below the meter and chart consisted of one very lame attempt at monetizing a blog with nothing but "Clement Hurd" as an anchor text link, linking to Google hot trends. When I searched on Google for "Clement Hurd" there was only one lonely AdWords ad on the right side bar. so this hot trend is not what I would call a money maker; let alone a money maker with some life left to it.

Now lets look at sample 2 - Jessica Simpson

How long is the hot trend likely to stay hot

This hot trend is listed all the way down in the number 12 position. And is only showing only "Spicy" on the Hotness Meter but when we look at the Google Search Volume index chart, we see Jessica Simpson as a hot trend had some other hear recently and this hot trend has not peaked yet.

Considering this hot trend has not peaked yet and Jessica Simpson is an internationally known singer and actress, even though the current Hotness is only spicy, the fact that this trend has not peaked yet makes it worth looking into a little deeper. So I go up to the Google Trends search field and type in Jessica Simpson. Guess what? The trends chart on this young lady show quite a few hot peaks within in the last year.

So I look at some of the news releases to see where this current spike came from. She was written up in the LA Times, Dallas Times Herald, E-Online and Hollywood.com. Unfortunately for here the write ups were about how she blew a performance in Grand Rapids. Still she is in the news now, has been quite a bit in the past and therefore probably will be again in the future. Having seen some things on T.V. about her recent inordinate amount of weight gain and her almost totally blowing a performance, I can almost count on her being in the news again in the very near future. Millions of people love to hear about and read about big stars falling from grace.

So what am I going to do to be made aware when anything having to do with Jessica Simpson surfaces online? I'm going to set a "Google Alert" on Jessica Simpson. Go to your Google Account home page and click on the "Alert" icon. I'll type in Jessica Simpson, set the type and how often I want to be alerted and have the alerts go to my Gmail account.

Google alerts will let me know before she hits hot trends again that she is in the news. This will allow me to go back to my records I'm keeping in Google Docs and quickly go to the previous information that made her hot and prepare a quick post about what maybe about to make her a hot trend again.

Then I do a Google web search for her name in quotes like this: "Jessica Simpson". Even with her name in quotes which cuts out Jessica only or Simpson only, there are still 29 MILLION results listed. On page one I find fan sites of her's that have PR-5 Google popularity ratings.

Now I have 2 reliable sources telling me the current information about her is hot, Google has shown her with some activity throughout "08" and she has been on Yahoo's chart for the last 689 days. Lookin good there Jessica.

Ok so you saw my steps to picking a hot trend in the last section and hopefully understood my rationale.

But lets take a minute here and talk about what's hot and not taking advantage of what it is because of how you personally feel about the hot trend or its subject.

The last thing you ever want to do is take some kind of opinionated approach as to whether or not a hot trend is worth building a project out of or not. In other words, regardless of what the hot trend is about, don't let your personal biases or opinions cloud your judgement as to whether or not you want to deal with any certain hot trends topic.

For example: I don't like pop music for the most part and country music even less. I have little respect for what I consider blonde bimboes that make it rich based Solely on their looks. Therefore as a rule I don't make it a habit to following anything that has to do with blonde bomb shell country singers. But there are such "Entertainers" that have audiences in the millions who have an interest in such entertainers.

I know if I can provide that massive audience with a little more information about their country star, on a blog that has been monetized with things on the same subject about the people the "Star" they are interested in, there is an extremely good chance that at least some of that audience can buy into my monetized items, and I will receive a commission for them. Guess what? I win! That's why I don't let my personal feelings about the subject of interest for a hot trend get in the way of me making money. I can't afford to.

The same thing applies to religion, politics, government, philosophy, business, foreign affairs or anything else all of us have our own opinions about. If you let your opinions stand in the way of making money, you won't make as much money with hot trends. PERIOD!

With that said, there is nothing that says you can't use your opinion, or voice your opinion as part of any hot trends project. Who knows; if your post on a hot trends project is well thought out, well written, delivers a rational argument about the hot trend, and is controversial to the norm regarding that hot trend, you may build traffic coming into that hot trends blog just to argue with you. I wouldn't waste a lot of time on doing so in the beginning though. But being controversial has made a lot of people a lot of money.

How You'll Make Money with Your Hot Trend Blog

Lets Complete Our Research On Jessica Simpson (This is a sample)

So how am I going to monetize this hot trend? What affiliate deals are available that caters to this Jessica Simpson fan audience that may appeal to them?

I'm going to run ads on my blog with my keyword rich post in it about this hot trend for people to click on and buy from a company I am affiliated with by virtue of an affiliate contract. You can become affiliated with hundreds of affiliate programs for free; however usually 4 or 5 will do along with Google Adsense.

I will provide links later where you can find tons of affiliate programs. Just remember, the more you are affiliated with, the more complicated your hot trends business becomes. You want to look for affiliate programs that can cover a wide range of products but still pay half way decent commissions.

I will not be expounding on the ins and outs of each affiliate program or how to work them. That is another project guide worth of information. Just remember, the simpler the system is to insert appropriate ads, the better for your business.

The only way you will learn which affiliate or Pay Per Click program (Like Google Adsense), to use with any given hot trend is by actually using them, testing them and keeping track of your testing.

The reason no one could possible teach you exactly which affiliate program will be best for which hot trend is the trends change in real time and the affiliate programs vary so much, as to the variables within each plan it is almost impossible to match the perfect affiliate, PPC or even CPA program with a hot trend. You will learn to develop and use your own judgement. However if you stick with these basic programs you can still make good money. The more you refine your process of matching hot trends with other ways of monetizing your hot trend blog, the more money you will make.

So here are some of the basic programs a lot of Internet marketers use:

Pay Per Click Systems

Allow you to earn money from relevant ads on your website
These ad services matches ads to your site's content and audience, and depending on the type of ad, you can earn money from clicks or impressions.

Google's Adsense (You definitely want to do this)

Adsense is the mirror image of Adwords, (The ads you see on the right side bar of a Google search result page.) Adwords ads are ads that are purchased ad space paid for on a per click basis by people with products to sell. Those same ads can appear in websites and blogs as Adsense ads.When those ads appear on our blogs, they are called Adsense and we make money on every click of those ads. It's that simple.

If you haven't signed up for a Google Adsense account yet, you may as well go ahead and do it now. Just go to your Google "My Account" page and click on the "Adsense" link under Products. Sign up, and come back to this section of the guide. IMPORTANT: When you sign up for Adsense, be sure to write down or copy and paste your publisher code to NotePad or put it in a document in your Google Docs. You're going to need it later.

Affiliate Programs

Amazon.com (Worth joining their affiliate program)

An example but not the best example, as their commission structure doesn't allow you to make much in the way of commissions. Still in some situations, they may be a good fit. In the case of Jessica Simpson I would certainly have links to her CD's page on amazon through my Affiliate link. To sign up go to: https://affiliate-program.amazon.com/

Ebay

The Ebay affiliate program can be a pretty good money maker depending on the type of system you choose. This program allows us to create a web site that features eBay auctions and receive anywhere from 50% on up to 75% commission on eBay revenue.

There are two ways that you can make money as an eBay affiliate:

1. Get people to sign up for eBay. You get $25 for each person that joins eBay by clicking a link on your site and then goes on to buy an item or win an auction on eBay in the next 30 days.
2. Get people to win eBay auction items from your site. You get up to 75% of what eBay makes on the auction. So, if your site is showing current listings for widgets and someone places a winning, $20 bid on a widget from your site, you would get anywhere from about $1.15 to $1.72 (50% - 75% of about $2.30). The percentage that you get depends on how much you have sold from your site. We're still in the 50% range.

Ebay is worth considering depending on the hot trend.

To sign up go to: https://www.ebaypartnernetwork.com

Those are probably the most well known. However there are many other affiliate programs you can match up with hot trends.

Other Affiliate Programs

Let's take seasonal hot trends for example. How about tax season. Did you know the people that sell "TurboTax", which is Intuit who also sells "Quicken" and "Quickbooks" and many other business software programs. Well you know something is going to be in the news about taxes especially considering the economic sewer we're all having to swim through right now.

I have put in a number of Google Alerts and can't wait for April the 15th just to see what I am going to have to name the blog for the hot trend on taxes. And guess what. I'm an affiliate for INTUIT. Guess what else. I already have my banner ad code ready to paste into the blog and the article written in a general enough way that I can plug in the hot trend word about taxes regardless of what they are.

To sign up go to: www.fi.intuit.com/marketing/affiliateprogram/

It really doesn't matter what hot trend keywords you are trying to find an affiliate program for, you can usually find one just by searching online. For example: Let's say the Super Bowl is coming up (It was really over this year just last week. Go Steelers!) So we do a Google Trends search on "Super Bowl"

There it is. Hot trends every year just like clockwork. So we want to be ready to jump on that as soon as the head lines start trending up. Usually around mid January. What if we could find a Sport Memorabilia affiliate program. Ok . . . good. We go to Google, and search on what? "Sport Memorabilia affiliate" and guess what pops up as number 1 in organic searches.
https://www.sportsmemorabilia.com/affiliate - with more pages right below it.

So my point here is; you can find an affiliate program that makes sense to use to monetize your hot trend blog with for just about any hot trend. Just think outside of the box and do some looking around. That's what Google is for, (Well in our case it's for a lot more but who's counting :o)

I'm going to take one more shot at you regarding monetizing your blog and then we'll move on. So in researching Jessica Simpson, when I just search on her name, only 2 AdWords ads come up in the side bar of the results page. Hmmmmm . . . not many people think she is much to advertise about . . . . or is she? Well she is a singer. What about Googling "Jessica Simpson CD". Curses, foiled again. Only 2 AdWords ads again.

So I'm going to go out on a limb here. It seems to me all these little singer/actress types under 40 (And yes some over 40), seem to have a line of fashions and accessories. So I Google "Jessica Simpson Fashions".

EUREKA! 3 pages of search results with AdWords Ads about Jessica Simpson Fashions.

So what does that tell me. Am I going to keyword my hot trend blog only about Jessica Simpson and her flop of a performance this hot trend was about. Well yes and no. That info will certainly be keyworded into the blogger blog name and in the first sentence. But then I want to remark about how the flopped performance combined her additional weight gain must be adversely affecting here Jessica Simpson fashion empire, and how it might be interesting to be a fly on the wall when her business manager tells Ms Jessica Simpson her fashion and Jessica Simpson fashion accessories business took a major hit, that percentage wise equals in loss to the Jessica Simpson Clothing and Accessory line what her current percentage of weight gain amounts to.

Is that mean? Who cares? I certainly don't. But I got the keywords in there that will have Google loading those Jessica Simpson Adwords ads into my blog like crazy. And if you think at least a couple of hundred plump little teenage girls that have nothing better to do than stay up on their hero that is going through the same shame they are with unwanted poundage, won't click on her Fashion AdSense ads on my blog, think again.

I happen to know how you can get another free tool I will direct you to later, that shows me the number one AdWords Ad buyer is paying a low of $00.41 to $01.21 per click through, (41 cents to a dollar & twenty one).

So lets say I wasn't writing this guide and actually took the time to load this hot trend. Because the visitors are so targeted, there is not only a potential of upwards of 2,000 visits on a hot trend like this, the potential that 10% of them would click through on an AdSense ad is pretty good as well. Now that's based on previous similar celebrity hot trends campaigns I've done. So lets see here . . . 200 click thru's X say 81 cents per click thru = $162.00 for what amounts to 1 hours work.

The research part of this hot trend set up took me all of 10 minutes. Will you be able to accomplish the same in as little time. Doubtful but you will with a little practice. Would you have known to search on this singer/actress beyond her name plus CD or the word movie? Maybe not! And if not you can probably see how you may have taken a pass on a hot trend that could have made you some serious money for one hours work. So you will have to think outside the box. Use your imagination and look beyond the obvious to cash in where others never will.

OK now that's just her fashions. What about posters? Sure there are all the 14 to 24 year young ladies that are fans but what about the 14 to 24 year old young men that have secretly (Or openly for that matter), lusted after Jessica Simpson. What if I went to AllPosters.com's affiliate site and signed up and found a killer poster of Jessica (Sans 40 pounds), and put a big poster of that little vixen right below my post.

Hello boys! Go ahead . . . click on Jessica. Now I don't consider myself sexist or exploitive. However just like every advertiser that uses a pretty girl or handsome hunk in an ad of any kind, I know that sex sells. And I have seen women wearing less than this in Vogue. So no judgements here please - Just think about the strategy I've employed that can allow me to tap into both the male and female market in this type of hot trend project.

By the way, you can sign up for "All Posters" at:
http://affiliates.allposters.com/affiliatesnet/

Open your mind. Use your imagination. Think outside the box. Google "Affiliate Program Directory". You'll find more affiliate programs than you ever wanted to know about.

Now let's get this hot little trend up on our blogger blog.

Blogging A Hot Trend

Lets say I chose the Jessica Simpson performance melt down in Grand Rapids hot trend.

I need to set up a blogger blog using keywords in my blog URL or web address. Some people call it a domain name but that is really only true if the blog is on my own domain instead of blogger's.

I know from additional research I want may want to include additional keywords in the blog title to take advantage of searches on other Jessica Simpson searches; i.e. clothes and fashions.

So I'm going for a title of "Jessica Simpson Fashions Weight Gain and Melt Down"

There for I will go for a blogger web address/URL of: JessicaSimpsonFashionsWeightGainMeltDown . . . . but blogger will only accept up to 36 characters. So I end up with this: JessicaSimpsonFashionsWeightGainMeltD - No big deal but keep yours under 36 characters if you can.

So I go to my Blogger Dashboard (Remember you bookmarked it in the Hot Trends tab). and copy and click on Create a Blog near the top right of the Manage Blogs section.

On the "Create a Blog" page as shown in screen shot ht-7 below I will do the 4 steps as indicated:

1. Paste or type in my Blog's title.

2. Paste or type in my Blog's Address/URL and check availability. If the address/URL is available you will see green text appear that says: This blog address is available. If the address is not available you will have to try again. Get inventive. Using hyphens (Dashes -) between your address/URL words will usually allow you to come up with an address that is available. The URL you select will be used by visitors, or yourself, to access your blog.

3. During the blog creation process, you'll have to select a URL for your blog if you want it hosted on Blog*Spot. Since there are already a large number of Blog*Spot blogs, you'll need to get creative and possibly try a few different ones before you find one that's available.One thing to note when selecting your blog's URL is that hyphens (also know as dashes, -) are the only non-alphanumeric characters allowed. Spaces aren't permitted, nor are underscores (_) or any other special characters.

4. Type in the Verification Word.

5. Click the "Continue Button.

Choose A Template

There are only a few basic templates to choose from. It doesn't matter. Just give it your best guess. Click a dot into the template of your choice then click the "Continue" button at the bottom of the page. On the next page, click on the "Start Blogging" button.

Hot Trend Blog Content

Your Blog Post - Entering Your Post

You can do something as simple as copying another blog post and
including a link to the post and then putting an opinion statement just
before and after the blog post you have an opinion on. In this case I
might type in above the post from the other blog something like:

"I don't think Jessica is being treated fairly in the following blog post".

Then use a little imagination to put other key words I'm wanting to go for
right after that opinion statement like; "Jessica may have weight
problems, and not giving the best performances she can right now, but
you have to admit with the line of Jessica Simpson clothing, apparel and
accessories line she has she is a pretty sharp business person.
Then another short statement below the post:

Then below the other blogs post, type in a short opinion statement about
how I would appreciate comments on my opinions.

However, I decided to write a short post about this girls woes as a
celebrity. This is not rocket science. Here's the post . . .

(SAMPLE) *Title:*
Poor Jessica Simpson with Weight Gain and Bad Performances -
Fashions and Accessories

Post:
Yes one of my favorite singing and acting stars, Ms Jessica Simpson
continues to be in the news about her weight problem, bad
performances and so on with headlines like:

* Jessica Simpson Performance Melt Down in Grand Rapids*
* Jessica Simpson's Weight Gain Makes Three Magazine Covers*
* Magazine Denies Dropping Simpson Over Weight Scandal*

I have no doubt Jessica Simpson's avid music fans like me will continue to buy her CD's but what about that large and previously profitable Jessica Simpson Fashion and Accessories line.

When the name sake Jessica Simpson herself probably can fit into any of the clothing items in her fashion line like the models do, I can't help but wonder what that is going to do to Jessica Simpson Fashion and Accessories Sales.

I think Jessica Simpson is just going through a rough patch in her life and will get it back together. With here CD sales tumbling, I hope this rough patch she's going through doesn't affect her clothing and fashion accessories business. What will Jessica have left then?

I know at least some people are still buying Jessica Simpson posters. My son just bought a poster of Jessica for his dorm room. I have to admit, when the girl was at her fashion weight, she was drop dead gorgeous. Maybe she needs a Jessica Simpson Poster in her clothing closet.

I hope she pulls herself out of this slump. Maybe I'll pay more attention to her career and let you know what I find here in this blog.

Denise

Nothing Fancy

See? Nothing fancy, just a quick 250 words that took me about 5 minutes. But look at the number of times I used the keywords: Jessica Simpson, Grand Rapids, Fashion, Accessories, clothing, posters, and so on. The blog address/URL, title, post title and keywords are what will be pulling in the targeted PPC ads (In this case we'll use Adsense), the site visitors should be clicking on.

Below the blog post editor field you will see a "Labels for your post" option field. This is where you want to type in your keywords. In this case I entered keyword phrases separated by commas like this: Jessica Simpson, Weight Gain, Grand Rapids Melt Down, Fashion Accessories, Poster

Then I clicked the "Publish Post" button. When you do your first few projects, you may want to just click the "Save Now" button if you want to save it for now so you can edit it later. When you do publish your post, you will come to a page that gives you the options to "View Post" or view it in a new window. Choose "In a new window". Proof read your post. If you have mistakes or find you want to make some changes, go back to the options page and click on the, "Edit post" link and make your changes. Then save the post.

Ok . . . my post is done. Total time less than 10 minutes.

Now go back to your blog dash board and fill in the blog for your hot trend description.

Now scroll down the page and answer the configuration question with the appropriate drop down options. Everything should be answered "YES" except for adult content and transliteration.

Now click the "SAVE SETTINGS" button at the bottom.

My methods and the strategies in this guide should start to make a lot of sense to you about now.

You may have noticed I'm not keeping any records as I set these things up. I will be going through record keeping when we go through the final walk through in the last chapter.

Let's move on to setting up our Adsense and poster ad.

Setting Up PPC And More

To run Pay Per Click (PPC) Ads on your blog, say AdSense for example, you need the code from the PPC Ad service, like AdSense placed into what is called a "Gadget" in your blog. The nice thing about using AdSence for your PPC Ad service is Blogger and Adsense are both owned by Google. So they make if very easy for you to set up your AdSence on a Blogger Blog.

From your hot trends blog dashboard, (Not your primary Dashboard that lists all your blogs), click on the "Lay Out" tab.

In the Lay Out screen you will see in the top right a link that says "Add Gadget". You will also see the same link below the post field. So there are 2 places you can add AdSense Ads through a Gadget. We will use the side bar gadget in this example. See screen shot ht-12 below:

When the "Add a Gadget" screen appears as a Pop Up, scroll down till you see the AdSense icon.

Click on the AdSense + icon. Another screen will appear. If you are not signed into your Adsense account, enter the e-mail address of your Gmail e-mail account and your zip code as you entered it when you signed up. You will then presented with the AdSense configuration screen.

Depending on where you are placing this AdSense Ad panel, you will use the drop down options to select the size, color, number of ads etc as seen below in screen shot ht-13. Notice that since I am putting the AdSense Ads in the side bar this time I used the tall and long or Sky Scraper ad that is 160 pixels in width by 600 pixels in height. You will need to play around with these a little to meet your personal preference.

NOTE: I don't believe you can put more than 2 set of AdSense ads on your blog. You can choose "Match Template" and the ads will be color coordinated with the Template you chose. As you look through the different size ads, the sample ads below the options will change accordingly.

When you have configured your ads, scroll to the bottom of the "Configure AdSense" screen and click on the "SAVE" button.

You can go through the process again and put another AdSense ad in the body of your post. OK your done. You will get to where you can accomplish this task in under 2 minutes.

You can use code generated from other PPC services by adding a Text Gadget and pasting the code into the Text Gadget. The same goes for affiliate ads you want to run with a hot trend.

Tracking your AdSense Click Thru's
go to your Google Adsense Account. Click on the "AdSense Setup" tab. On the next screen click on the "Channels" tab.

On the next screen click on URL channels.

Now click on "Add new URL channels."

Now where it says "Enter URLs to track, one per line:" paste in your blog's URL.

Then click on the "Add channels" button. Now in reports you will be able to see what kind of impressions (site visits), you are getting, and how many click thru's you're getting.